T0359357

DUNNIES
LOOS and
LONGDROPS

ZANY, RAMSHACKLE, IMPROBABLE AND EXTRAORDINARY PLACES TO GO

Douglass Baglin & Yvonne Austin

A lovely bunch of coconuts

The giggle house

Barrier start! – they're off!

4 – u – 2 – p

The big flush

Name your poison

I feel a perfect arse

For tail ends at Woodend

The log bog

Slow motion

Holey trinity

Well-defended ladies

The greatest show on earth

Watch out for the hangover

Explosive situation

**Flash flushing
system**

Hot seat

Wow – that mustard's hot!

Doctor Who!

Two holer

Lady in waiting

For longruns

For short ones

For tapered ones

For pretty ones

Beer comes out here!

Something brewin!

Big D

Hoo-ray and up she rises!

For geyser gazers

Meeting house

Bach with a loo to match

All bottled up!

Beach box

What about the men?

For ladies on the hop

For gents with the trots

Bed-sitter

For retiring ladies

For those in need of
a charge

Bay of plenty

A call of distress

Busting to go!

Letting off steam

The last drop

For round heads

Sailors' horn pipe

Wind sock

Stag party

Clutha's closet

Authors' picture

For country bum-kins

Show passports please

Earthquake proof

My aim is true

Sneaky leakie!

The big wind

Timber!

Grand Parade

Underground
Movement

Hanging rail

Taj mahal

Are you a happy camper?

L. P. G. filling centre

Gin slings

Pisa house

Don't worry _ it will all blow over

Castaway

Book here for organ performance

Free hot water

Wind proof

First published in Australia in 1984
by Child & Henry Publishing Pty Ltd

This edition published in 2019 in Australia
by New Holland Publishers

Sydney • Auckland

newhollandpublishers.com

Level 1, 178 Fox Valley Road, Wahroonga,
2076 Australia

5/39 Woodside Ave Northcote, Auckland
0627 New Zealand

Copyright © 2019 New Holland Publishers

A record of this book is held at the National
Library of Australia.

ISBN 9781760791117

Group Managing Director: Fiona Schultz
Production Director: Arlene Gippert
Printer: Toppan Leefung Printing Limited